IN A HEARTBEAT

ALSO BY
PAMELA WALKER-WILLIAMS

Promise of a Rainbow: Poetry

Marian of Memphis
*(A LETTER FOR MY MOTHER,
EDITED BY NINA FOX)*

COMING SOON

Spiritual Gifts

In a Heartbeat

PAMELA WALKER-WILLIAMS

STILETTO PRESS PUBLISHING | TEXAS

2014

Compilation Copyright © 2014 Pamela Walker-Williams
Stiletto Press Publishing
2951 Marina Bay Dr., Suite 130
League City, TX 77573

All Rights Reserved.
Printed in the United States of America.

No part of this publication by be reprinted, stored in a retrieval system, or transmitted in a form without prior permission of the publisher.

Some of the poems in this collection were published as:

In a Heartbeat (Xceptional Creations Publishing) - 1993
A Brand New Me -1992
Refections of Pam - 1978

Second Edition

10 9 8 7 6 5 4 3 2

ISBN-10:0982890923
ISBN-13:978-0-9828909-2-9

Library of Congress Catalog Card Number 93-94999

Layout Designed by: PW2 Design

Cover Illustration by: lay, © 2014
Used under license from Shutterstock Images LLC

Text Edited by: Jan Emanuel-Costley,
Administrative Consulting Services

Dedication

This book is a quilt of my life experiences. Therefore, I find it only fitting to dedicate it to all the people who have contributed a patch to my quilt.

Especially,

Marian, Ruffus, and Kameron

Our heart is our most vital organ; and although scientifically we don't think or feel with our hearts, emotionally we do. When things are funny we feel lighthearted, when things are sad, we have heavy hearts. Our hearts go out, they break, they are cold, they are soft, and they ache. Our hearts are the keys to our souls and the doors of our spirit.

It is within my heart where this collection originated. Some of these poems are as old as my soul, where others are as new as my dreams. Everyone in my life has inspired me to write something and it gives me great pleasure to share with you...

In a Heartbeat

Contents

A Free Heart ... 9

For Sweethearts ... 15

My Broken Heart Still Beats ... 21

Lighthearted ... 29

With A Heavy Heart ... 37

A Heart Filled with Praise ... 43

My Heart Sings ... 53

Heart Felt ... 59

P. WALKER-WILLIAMS

A Free Heart

A Simple Thanks Won't Do

How do you thank someone for
The Encouraging things they say?
For the loving smile they give you
As you go from day to day?

How do you let them know
That they mean the world to you?
That you cherish their friendship
And respect all that they do?

How do you show someone
All the gratitude you hold?
When they've enriched your life and
Helped you achieve your goals?

Well, you are that someone
And a simple thanks won't do.
For my friend you are God sent.
So I thank God for sending you.

(A Brand New Me, 1992)

I'm Glad My Friend is You

As we grow older the patterns change
Of all the things we do.
And it's so hard to find a friend
Who really cares for you.
A friend stands by you through thick and thin
No matter what you do.
And I'm so glad that I have a friend
And I'm glad my friend is you.

No matter who you are
You can't survive alone.
And if you ever try
Something will go wrong.
I'm glad I have a friend,
And I'm glad my friend is you.

Wherever you go people talk a lot.
You know their main concern
Is what you have or haven't got
It's really good to have
A concerned friend that's true.
And I'm so glad that I have a friend
And I'm glad my friend is you.

(REFLECTIONS OF PAM, 1978)

P. WALKER-WILLIAMS

Old Friends

Football Games and Homecoming Queens
Majorettes and Proms it all seems
Like such a lifetime ago, just like a dream.
When did we grow up? A changing scene.

You were there when I needed you.
Touched my heart
And helped to see me through
All of those growing pains and joys
As if you knew
Time slipped by together we both grew.

Summer days and picnics in the park,
Rushing home from play when it got dark.
We've put our jump ropes
And play things away.
To realize tomorrow is today.

Years gone by, yet time has been our friend.
I thank God our friendship never ended.
Whenever fire flies shine or
Stars fall from the sky
I'll make a wish and think of you and I.

Old Friends, We reminisce the past
Old Friends, Too bad it could not last.

Old Friends,
It's sad and that's no lie.
When old friends have to part
And say good-bye.

Jesus Made Us Sisters

Years ago when you were born
So very far away,
God had made a plan
For us to celebrate this day.

Even though we both grew up
So many miles apart,
He led us to each other
By touching both our hears.

I treasure our friendship
A blessing from above
For Jesus made us sisters,
When Jesus gave us love.

P. WALKER-WILLIAMS

For Nurturing Him

Thank you for the baby
That you nourished through the years.

Thank you for the toddler
Who you wiped away his tears.

Thank you for the little boy
That you have watched to grow.

Thank you for the teenager
Whom the world you help to show.

Thank you for the young adult
That you lovingly shared with me.

Thank you for the wonderful man
That my husband grew to be.

For Sweethearts

There is My Love

There are no boundaries to my love.
There is no way to contain it.
It constantly flows
Always replenished.
It is as close as my heart,
And as distant as the farthest star.

There are no stipulations to my love.
It comes with no conditions.
It's full of hope
Always trusting.
It is as soft as my gentle touch,
And as firm as your deepest belief.

There is no end to my love.
It's infinite and everlasting.
Changing directions, always encompassing
It is as fresh as the morning dew
And as ancient as the evening sky.
Seen on the surface
Yet hidden in the soul.
Silent in presence
Yet loud in declaration.
Free in spirit
Yet enslaved in an embrace.
Mine to bestow
Yet yours alone to have and to hold.

This Day You Wed

This day you wed, your life will change
You two shall become one.
Engulfed by one another's love
Your new life has just begun.

This day you vow eternal trust
Forever and always.
The world is yours to have and hold
Beginning on this day.

This day you start to face the world
And the obstacles it bears.
You'll draw from one another's strength
And commitment that you share.

This day you web, before God you stand
Presented as bride and groom.
To each other you must submit
This day you "*Jump the Broom.*"

(THIS POEM WAS WRITTEN FOR
MY WEDDING ANNOUNCEMENT)

To Think of Him

To think of him, warms my heart
With thoughts that last all day.
Thoughts that are the clinging kind
And grow when he's away.

To think of him, soothes my soul
Thoughts of his warm embrace.
To look at me you'd never know
That he had left his trace.

To think of him, eases my mind
A love I feel is there.
He reassures me constantly
With tender loving care.
To think of him, renews myself
And sets my soul aflame.
I hope and pray every night
That he feels the same.

To think of him, is my life
For my love is his to keep.
My life is built around him,
My feelings towards him are deep.
Think of him? I always do.
I hope he thinks of me.
Perhaps he does, I always will
Think of him constantly.

(APRIL 26, 1975)

Never Give Up Hope

Never live a life
Not designed for you.
Planning, hopes and dreams
For these things don't come true.

Never try to love
A love not meant to be.
So don't hold him tight
For it's not meant to be.

These are some old tales
Longing to be told.
Tales told to the young
Tales told by the old.

Never give up hope
Just because of fear.
Never do believe
Everything you hear.

(January 12, 1983)

P. WALKER-WILLIAMS

My Broken Heart Still Beats

Goodbye

Now as we go our separate ways
Finding fault yet finding praise.
There's one thing left to be said
We still have our lives to be lived ahead.

Saying Goodby is always hard.
Sorrow felt as love ones part
The questioning to what fate holds –
The emptiness inside my soul.

Wonderful memories that we share
Of times together, time spent with care
These images
I will forever keep
To help me smile
Even though I weep.

(August 16, 1982)

Will He Care?

The familiar voice that answers the phone,
That is no longer there.
The faint fragrance of perfume,
That's absent from the air.
The things that remind him of me are gone,
I wonder, will he care?

Will he care the pet names he hates to be called
Aren't spoken anymore?
Will he care that this smiling face
Won't greet him at the door?
Will he care that I'm not the one
Who warms him when he's cold?
Will he care that this part of his life
Is gone forever more?

The familiar kiss that's soft and moist,
That he'll no more receive.
The warm embrace that soothes him so,
That's gone this time indeed.

My name not spoken from his lips
Will he miss the sound?
No longer at his beckon call
For I won't be around.
Insignificant me... gone.
And gone to who knows where?
And one thing that I'll never know is
Did he really care?

P. WALKER-WILLIAMS

Tears of Love

I weep on my pillow every night
Because my love is strong.
I long for him to hold me tight
If he was right or wrong.

I cry sometimes unconsciously,
Because I love him so.
And when he feels he hurt me,
He'll somehow let it show.
Tears of love can be from joy,
New experiences together.
Experiences that we enjoy,
And will remember forever.

Tears of love are all kinds,
They drop, they roll, they flow.
They come from thoughts from
Heart and mind,
And they'll refuse to go.
The best part of the crying tears,
I needlessly must say.
Is when he hugs away my fears,
And kisses my tears away.

(1975)

One More Time

I've been here before,
Yes, I know what it's like.
You'll play the music soft,
Then we will kiss by candlelight.

I don't know exactly how I should feel...
Is it all make believe or is it real?

What's that you say?
It will be different this time.
You'll turn the lights down low,
And then fill my glass with wine.

I only hope that I am not living in a dream...
And that this is as wonderful as it seems.

So, I'll try one more time.
Can it really hurt to try one more time?

I'll try one more time.

Please don't let me down this time.

P. WALKER-WILLIAMS

Left Behind

I'm always the one who gets left behind,
And yes I wonder why?
Hurt and sorrow fill my heart
And tears flow from my eyes.
I'm always the one they tell "chin up"
You'll find another man.
I'm always the one who gets left behind,
And I don't understand.

I'm always the one who gets the worst end
Out of every deal.
I'm always the one whose insides turn out
As if I do not feel.
I'm always the one who gets
the pat on the back,
When they say that it is over.
I'm always the one who has the bad luck,
Who never found a four leaf clover.

I'm always the one who really cares,
To love him and fill his needs.
I'm always the one who lost the battle
The one who did not succeed
I'm always the one who will try again.
Praying that things will go right.
I'm always the one left in the dark
Who didn't see the light.

Yes me, I'm the one who gets left behind,
The one love never finds.
I am the one whose heart got broke,
Yes, really broke this time.

(MARCH 5, 1975)

IN A HEARTBEAT

P. WALKER-WILLIAMS

P. WALKER-WILLIAMS

My Yard is Full of Leaves
(And I don't even have a tree)

My friend it really takes a lot
For you to anger me.
But my yard is full of leaves
And I don't even have a tree.

There's nothing much I can do
To stop the wind from blowing.
So your leaves drift into my yard
Each day without me knowing.

When I have to rake them,
To put them in the trash,
Low and behold here come your cats
Making the garbage dash.

It's not that I dislike cats,
I really think they are fine.
But I just don't not understand
Why you must have nine.

How often do your cats have liters,
Why don't you get them fixed?
Everywhere I step or look
There's a reminder of your kits.

IN A HEARTBEAT

No, you may not park your car
Behind mine in my drive.
Your driveway has four parking spaces,
My drive does not make five.

I can't back out my driveway anyway,
Your branches block my view.
Plus I'm afraid I'll smash a cat,
Just if and when I do.

I like you as a neighbor.
I hope that you'll agree.
But soon I plan to get an ax,
And chop down that damn tree.

(JANUARY 2, 1995)

Are We There Yet

The luggage is packed,
The chicken is fried,
And we are ready to start on our way.
To Grandmamma's house
Let the journey begin!
A trip that will take us all day.

First we stop for some gas
Before we get on the road,
At the store that is right down the street.
We fill up the tank
Get back in the car
When I hear, "

Is it time to eat?

One hour goes by,
And we're making good time,
When the children notice a jet,
Flying high in the sky,
At the speed of sound.
When I hear

Are we there yet?

IN A HEARTBEAT

I explain once again,
About distance and time,
And that Grandmamma lives very far.
Then I see my son doing that
"I need to go" dance,
So I stop, and we pile out of the car.

I get back on the road,
With one goal in mind
And that is, to make it by dark.
Then I realize that
It's just the crack of dawn.
So on with my mission I embark.

Then I hear this scream
A sure cry of death
I step on the brakes just to see.
What would make this sound?
Come out of my child's mouth?
And he says

She keeps touching me!

Now my nerves have been pluck,
Stepped on, and abused.
For it is hard to be super mom.
(What made me have kids?
Had I just lost my mind?)

All of a sudden I heard a yarn.
They were taking a nap,
So I stepped on the gas,
I was starting to make good time.
If they would just sleep
Through the entire trip,
Then this journey would surely be fine.
But alas they awake,

And start searching for food.
For it was now time to eat lunch.
(A half a day down, and one half to go.)
They found and began to munch.

They start playing games,
"I spy something blue"
They name everything they could guess.
"Is it the sky? The flowers? The wall?
Hey mom,

Are we there yet?

They nap, they eat, they fuss, they fight.
But I continue to drive.
Into the sunset
Towards Grandmamma's house
For that's where my sanity lies.

(Disney World Trip 1992)

One Day

One day I'm going to write a poem
And dedicate it to a friend.
It's gonna' rhyme and everything
With a beautiful beginning and end.

I'll take it to a publisher
(If that's where all poems go.)
I'll make a million dollars,
At least I do hope so.

People all over will read my poem,
It'll be in magazines too!
Another million dollars,
Now for me that's two.

And when I am a millionaire
With my two million you see,
I'm gonna' write another poem
And then I'll have me three.

(1973)

P. WALKER-WILLIAMS

With a Heavy Heart

P. WALKER-WILLIAMS

A Poem for My Brother

It's been a long time,
Since I wrote a poem
It seems I had nothing to say.
But now it is time,
And I've picked up my pen,
For this has always been my way.

To address world affairs
Or the state of my mind,
I have found it most fitting to write.
But what must one do,
Where there is nothing to say,
And you stare at blank paper all night.

What caused me to stop?
Just what shut me down?
Why did I run and take cover?
Perhaps I was worn out,
Perhaps I got tired,
Or was it the loss of my brother?

My brother's passing was quite a shock,
To lose him so early in life.
He left behind my mother and I,
His two young kids and a wife.

But why is he gone?
Why take his life?
He was just beginning to live.
He had found God,
And repented his sins
He had so much more to give.

We can't pick the time,
Or place of our death
For only God knows where and when.
God found it fitting to call Terry home,
But one day I'll see him again.

So again I shall write.
Yes, I've picked up my pen
To comment on one thing or another.
But before I begin,
I have something to say.
So I've written this poem for my brother.

(TERRY THOMAS, 1962-1986)

P. WALKER-WILLIAMS

Why So Young?

"Why so young?" we always ask,
When a young friend passes away.
Why couldn't it be someone old?
Someone who lived their day.

She barely saw the sun rise,
And hardly saw the moon.
But now she's gone far beyond,
It seems she left too soon.

No one ever sent her flowers
That she could smell or touch.
'Til she could no longer see them,
Or love them half as much.

We seem to think she didn't know life.
But that's where we were wrong.
She lived her life entirely,
Until all of it was gone.

I'll always love her memory,
And thoughts of her I'll keep.
I think about her often,
Sometimes I'll even weep.

I pray to God one sincere wish,
And this to you I'll tell.
May I love life as my friend did,
And cherish it as well.

(JEANETTE LAVERN FISHER -1957 -1975)

It is Not the End

It's through God's word
That we are nourished
As a tree through its roots
We grow as we flourish.

Shedding our bodies
Whenever God calls,
As a tree sheds its leaves
Each year in the fall.

To awake in Heaven,
God's Praises to Sing!
As a tree reawakens
And blooms in the Spring.

So rest assure,
It is not the end.
For God will start life,
All over again.

It is the Beginning...

P. WALKER-WILLIAMS

A Heart Filled With Praise

I WILL PRAISE THE, O LORD WITH MY WHOLE HEART; I WILL SHOW FORTH ALL THY MARVELOUS WORDS. (PSALM 9:1)

Paradise

As he lifted His head hanging on the cross
At a place called Calvary.
He whispered words
for the world to hear
"Thou'll be in Paradise with Me."
Then the darkness came,
And the sky went dark
His spirit He did commend.
Then our Savior died,
That day on the cross
Thus allowing us to live.

We rejoice in knowing that He lives.
And He waits for us in Paradise.
What a wonderful reason to give
Your life to Christ
For He died, so we could live.

Come and walk with Him, on the waters deep
Let us all step out on faith.
Just as Peter did, with his eyes on Christ
Just resting your whole weight.
With faith the size of a mustard seed
We can move the mountains high.

Won't you come with us
as we walk with Christ
And we'll meet in Paradise.

For a Child was born in Bethlehem
On a cold winter's eve.
Wrapped in swaddling clothes
in a manger far
For the whole world to receive.

Yes, the Child was Christ,
and the world was change.
And we'll never be the same

Accept Jesus Christ as your Savior and
Be in Paradise with Him.

We rejoice in knowing that He lives.
And He waits for us in Paradise.
What a wonderful reason to give
Your life to Christ
For He died, so we could live.

*AND WHEN JESUS HAD CRIED
WITH A LOUD VOICE, HE SAID,
FATHER, INTO THY HANDS I COMMEND MY SPIRIT:
AND HAVING SAID THUS, HE GAVE UP THE GHOST.
(LUKE 23:46)*

P. WALKER-WILLIAMS

This is All That You Have to Do

You're feeling down, and I understand
I wish there was something that I could do
To make you feel better or just help you smile.
So I've written this poem just for you.

To let you know that you are not alone,
And that God really does care.
To let you know that I am your friend,
And that I will always be here.

Just whisper a prayer,
When things get too rough.
Call on Jesus and He'll see you through
All of the bad times, as well as the good.
This is all that you have to do.

Reflect on your life,
And the people you've touched
All of us who call you our friend.
You've enriched other's lives,
With a sincere friendship
And a caring that never does end.

Sometimes things go wrong,
And they always do,
But it's all a part of God's plan.
Just hold your head high
Keep the Lord in your life,
And remember that you have a friend.

(A Brand New Me, 1992)

Jesus is There

When life gets too rough
And it seems like a lot to bear...
When all hope seems lost
And you feel as if no one cares...
When you continue to pray
And you wonder if God hears...
Jesus is there,
Praise the Lord!

Thank Him for His Son,
Who died in our place
Thank Him for your Children,
Thank Him for His Grace.

Thank Him for your life,
And all He's done for you
But never give up hope,
For God will see you through.

He will see you through,
The rough times and your pain.
He will give you hope,
Sunshine despite the rain.
He'll answer all your prayers
Your life He'll rearrange
He is always there,
Praise the Lord!

He Answers Prayer

When I laid in my mother's womb
My mother prayed for me.

Afraid that I'd grow up to soon

My mother prayed for me.
My mother sent me off to school
She taught me the golden rule.

Isn't it good to know?
Jesus, He loved me so
Even when I didn't care
He answered my mother's prayer.

There are people who live in the streets
Please Lord look after them.

Children dying from no food to eat
We've got to pray for them.

So many people hooked on dope
People discouraged, lost all hope.

Help them Lord they don't know
That You love them so.
They need to know you Care
And that you always answer prayer.

Jesus will meet you where you are.
But He cares too much for you
To leave you there.

I know the road seems rough
And sometimes unfair
But you can rest reassured,
That He answers prayer.

Isn't it good to know?
Jesus loves us so
No matter when or where
He always answers prayer.

Whose Day is it Anyway?

The Christmas lights are all about
The carolers, they sing and shout
The children trim the Christmas tree
There are gifts for you and me

Santa will make his rounds tonight.
But something about this
is just not right.
I only have one thing to say,

Whose day is it anyway?

The air is full of Christmas smells.
The Christmas stories – the people tell
The children's laughter fills the air,
The relatives they are all there.
People kiss under the mistletoe,
I can't help but wonder if they know
So to them I say...

Whose day is it anyway?

Let's put Jesus, back in our Christmas!
Not just once a year but
Each and every day that we live.
He's the reason for the season
Our praise to Him we give!

For he bled for me, back on Calvary
Yes He died for me, People can't you see
That He's real, you know
And we need Him So
You just can't let go
Of our Savior So
To you I say...

Whose day is it anyway!

P. WALKER-WILLIAMS

*And we know that all things
work together for good
to them that love God,
to them who are the called
according to his purpose.
(Romans 8:28)*

My Heart Sings

Just the Same

I don't know, what cause the wind to blow.
But the winds' gonna' blow just the same.
Don't know why there's stars up in the sky.
But the stars twinkle there just the same.

Oh - I don't know how you
can falsely accuse me
of not loving you when I do.

But there's one thing that I do know
That I'll never will let you go.
No, I'll never, no never let you go.

Can't explain, what causes it to rain.
But it rains and it pours just the same.
I can't tell what makes it sleet and hail.
But it falls from the sky just the same.

Don't know what causes the wind to blow..
Wonder why the stars are in the sky...
Can't explain why it rains..
Can't tell why it hails...

There's one thing that I'm sure of
That's my everlasting love
And I never, no never let you go.

(REFLECTIONS OF PAM, 1978)

Send You a Dream

If only I could send you a dream,
Oh how real I'd make it seem.
With you loving me,
And me loving you.
No reason why this can't be true.

It has been so hard for me,
to find the words
To capture the love that I feel.
But if I could send you a dream,
Then afterwards
You would know...

I long for you, every night
And every day you are away.
And in that dream, you'll realize
For us there is no other way.

Than in each other's arms,
We'll find a way
To capture the love that we feel.
So pretend I sent the dream,
So afterwards
You will know...

That heaven is when I'm in your arms
Yes heaven is when, I'm in your arms.

(April 22, 1981)

Reflection of my Destiny

Looking at the inner most
Message in your soul
Is like reading an image from my mind.
Like seeing a reflection of my destiny,
Like looking through the window at time.

Chorus
Our love is like a mirror, showing me
Things I can feel but are so hard to see.
You're my mirror, my image,
My soul and my mind
A reflection of my destiny.

People often wonder where they're headed to
For what purpose in life are they here?
Some just grow older, others grow colder
Then there are those like you and me.

The love that we share has reached a plane that's unknown,
A merging no words can explain.
You can see in me, I can feel in you
More than a love is exchanged

Repeat Chorus

(1977)

Time Goes By

See if life cares what your moods are.
See if wishful thinking gets you very far.
Hopes and Dreams
Are just things you see
Until you let them out.

I remember when you were a part of me.
Life for me then was as happy as can be.
But since then
Don't know when I'll be
Back in touch with you.

Don't know if I want to see you anymore.
For all I know, things could be like before.
Time goes by,
That's no lie my dear.
Since you shut me out.

Reality,
Try to deal with it.
A Possibility
You'll have to live with it.
No Catastrophe,
Just a fool,
Who was in love with you.

I Didn't Even Try

He's left me before, I know
I let him walk out of my life.
It's different this time it's so...
So for real.

I didn't even try this time.
I never even said one word.
And no, I didn't cry this time,
It's for real.

No, I just don't need him no more,
And at last I am free.
I politely closed the door
To be me.

It's gonna be hard at first
To get my direction clear.
But things could be a whole lot worse.
He could still be here.

I didn't even try this time.
I never even said one word.
I helped him pack his bag this time
He's left my world.

HeartFelt

P. WALKER-WILLIAMS

Another Day in My Life

Hey mister, save that cardboard for me.
This can be my shelter from the storm,
You see.
Please don't throw that food away,
It can help me last just one more day.
I have no home
I have no place to go.
I walk the streets, even though I know...
Tomorrow for me has no meaning.
It's just another day in my life.

I'll wash your windows,
Get them really clean.
All I want is some change,
Please don't be so mean.
I want a job, but no one will hire me.
I'm homeless, no phone or address you see.
I have no home,
No place to lay my head.
I have no life, might as well be dead...
Yesterday for me has no memories.
It's just another day in my life.

Hey lady, I have a college degree!
I had a great job, and a house you see.
Then they had this layoff,
And my job was gone.

Had no money saved, just a car, and a loan.
I have no home,
No place to rest my feet.
I'm all alone, no matter who I meet...
Today for me has no hope.
It's just another day in my life.

Hey Senator, I've got two babies you see,
Living in the streets, is no place to be.
From school to school,
Trying to educate them,
Trying to keep them honest,
Please don't forsake them.
I'm not on welfare,
Just trying to survive.
Just another mother trying to keep her kids alive.

I have no home,
No place to bathe.
My life seems worthless,
but I want my kids' lives saved.

Yesterday, Today, and Tomorrow
Are all the same to me.
It's just another day in my life.

(1992 – Reflections of Pam)

Teachers

We entrust you with our children,
Each and every day.
You share their joys and sorrows,
You shape and mold the clay.

You listen when they need you,
You talk and teach them so.
You're always there to guide them
For this we love you so.

With you they'll develop memories
For future years to come.
You're building the foundation
From where our new leaders will come.

(1993)

*Train up a child in the way he should go;
even when he is old he will not depart from it.
(Proverbs 22:6)*

People of the Nile

I hear my ancestors calling
Across time and many miles.
A proud and mighty people.
The People of the Nile.

My Soul has traveled far
Through millenniums to be
The essence of greatness
The people that you see.

My forefather came from many
Faraway lands, Nubia, Egypt, Kush,
Monroe and the Sudan.

Kashta was a great ruler
As were Planky and Shabaka.
And written in the Bible
Are tales of Tirhakah.

Our history is older
Than recorded time.
A strong and regal people
Your ancestors and mine.
When you faced with a struggle
And feel like it's something you can't do
Remember the rich history
Of someone great just like you.

My Essence

I have been a part of your life
Since the beginning of time.
The day the world was created
You became a part of mine.

So millions of years then passed
And our existence came to be.
Through light-years, space and time,
You finally came to me.

I didn't need to see you,
To know that you were there.
I didn't need to question,
How soon I came to care.

And so our lives united,
A destiny came true.
On this special day in time,
I give all my love to you.

(For Kameron, January 12, 1983)

ABOUT THE AUTHOR

Pam Walker-Williams was born in Chicago, but moved to Memphis at an early age. In Memphis, Pam attended the Booker T. Washington High School and the University of Memphis.

Pam later moved to Houston, TX where she married, had one son, worked at the NASA Johnson Space Center, and earned a Master's Degree in Digital Media from the University of Houston - Clear Lake.

Pam owns and operates "The Page-Turner Network" where she is recognized by the literary community as one of the country's top web designers. She is a member of Alpha Kappa Alpha Sorority, Inc., The Good Book Club, and a volunteer and supporter of Divas For A Cure, Inc.

She resides in Texas with her husband Ruffus.

AUTHOR'S NOTE

The first poem I remember writing was entitled "Mexico". I was in Mrs. Pritchards's 6th grade class. It wasn't my first crack at poetry, however it is the first poem that I can still recall *(well sort of...)*

> *Mexico is the place to go*
> *When you are out on a tour*
> *Or vacation or so.*

That's where my memory fails me. But if I recall correctly, it was a snappy little poem.

I wrote poetry all through elementary, Middle School, and High School. Some I remember *(because I wrote them down)* but many I don't. It was in college that I started putting music to my poems. The first song I wrote was "Reflection of my Destiny" which is included in this collection.

Since college I have published three books of poetry, written several children's plays, owned a dance studio (*Hip Bones in Motion*), published book marks, and greeting cards. Thank you so much for reading my work.

I appreciate you.

ACKNOWLEDGEMENTS

A Very Special Thank you goes to:

*My **Family** for Foundation*
Johnson, Walker, & Williams Clans

*My **Sorors** for Encouragement*
Debra, Paulette, Nina & Pat

*My **Girl-Friends** for Inspiration*
Wanda, Deon, Eddgra, Juanita, Shelley, Jetola & Jan

*My **PageTurner.net** Family*
Especially Bernice, Victoria, Eric,
Jewell, Victor & Kimberla

The Good Book Club

My Hip Bone In Motion Kids

In Loving Memory of My Friend
Karan Latimer

The End

www.ingramcontent.com/pod-product-compliance
Lightning Source LLC
Chambersburg PA
CBHW020021050426
42450CB00005B/585